Rhythm Rescue!

Musical Activities to Expand Rhythmic Vocabulary

BY LYNN M. BRINCKMEYER

SHAWNEE PRESS
EXCLUSIVELY DISTRIBUTED BY
HAL•LEONARD®
7777 W. BLUEMOUND RD. P.O. BOX 13819 MILWAUKEE, WI 53213

In Australia Contact:
Hal Leonard Australia Pty. Ltd.
4 Lentara Court
Cheltenham, Victoria, 3192 Australia
Email: ausadmin@halleonard.com.au

Visit Shawnee Press online at **www.shawneepress.com**
Visit Hal Leonard online at **www.halleonard.com**

Table of Contents

Purpose of the Book

Rhythm is comprised of various lengths of sounds and silences over a basic pulse or beat. **Duration** is another term that is used to describe the length of a sound. The backbone of any piece of music we perform is the rhythmic foundation. One of the biggest challenges for singers is being able to see and immediately reproduce a correct rhythm. Singers are often accused of less than accurate rhythmic integrity and this book can help students develop strong internal clocks.

A variety of strategies can be useful when learning, or fine tuning, rhythms. All of the exercises and suggestions in this book are intended to expand the rhythmic vocabulary of singers. I have learned that students of all ages, from the very young through university students, are more successful if they use a physical gesture during the learning process. We do not have a lever, a bow, strings or buttons to push. Consequently, using physiology helps solidify those rhythms in the body. The more opportunities singers have to develop a personal relationship with various rhythmic patterns, the more comfortable they become. Our ultimate goal is to have our students eventually internalize the pulse. As they develop that skill, it may be useful to have a student keep the beat on a drum, or use a metronome, when the students are engaged in the activities outlined in this book. Periodically, the teacher is instructed to provide cards with different rhythmic values. If rhythm cards are not available, the rhythms can be printed by hand on inexpensive paper plates.

This book is set up in two different sections: **Isolated Rhythm Activities** and **Rhythms with Pitch or Text**. Many of the songs included in the second section, Rhythms with Pitch or Text, include traditional folk songs. Using these traditional melodies to teach rhythm concepts provides an additional vehicle to expose our students to the folksongs of our country. Even though the book is not intended to be a sequential curriculum, teachers may find it useful to start at the beginning of this book and proceed in chronological order, and move through the exercises by introducing one for each new day of rehearsal. Conversely, bouncing around and selecting different exercises that support the rhythmic concepts in the music that is being studied at that time can be just as effective.

All of the strategies in this book are intended to support the required curriculum and state and national music standards in different settings. Most of these activities can be used with different songs in the book; in other words, they are interchangeable. They can also be transferred to barred instruments, non-pitched percussion instruments and performance literature the students are studying.

These ideas are meant to spark creativity to match up to what students need. Take any of the tactics and build upon them, modify and adapt to whatever is needed to get the students successfully reading and creating rhythms. Enjoy!

Rhythm Elements

Rhythmic Elements	Rhythmic Name
	ta
	ta-di
	ta-a
	ta-ka-di-mi
	ta-di-mi
	ta-ka-di
	ta-mi
	ta-ka

MAKE A SOUND - MAKE A RHYTHM

Teaching Ideas

- Display different rhythm values on the board.
  - Example: quarter note, eighth note, quarter rest, two 8th notes, etc.

- Invite students to create rhythm sounds using body percussion.
  - They will create a different sound for each note or rest value.
  - Example: stomp for quarter notes, snap for eighth notes.
- Display a rhythm pattern similar to the one pictured here.
  - Have students pair up and teach their newly created body percussion to their partner.
  - Allow time for both students to teach their partner.
- Keep the same note and rest values and place them in a different order.
  - Tell the students to clap the new patterns together at the same time.
  - Have them add body percussion again to the new pattern.

Advanced Extensions

- Encourage students to join both of the body percussion patterns together to make one long rhythmic phrase.
- Allow time for the students to review the body percussion for the new extended rhythmic pattern.
- Invite students to perform their rhythms for the class.
  - Have all of the students perform their individual rhythm patterns as you go through the class by rows, or around a circle.
- Finally, have all of the students perform their individual patterns all at the same time.

Rhythm Round the Circle

Teaching Ideas

- Have students stand in a circle.
- The teacher performs a 4-beat rhythm pattern using body percussion.
  - Example: Ta, ta-di, ta-di, ta.

- The student next to the teacher repeats the same pattern, using the same body percussion.
  - Reinforce the idea that sometimes a student may perform a rhythm pattern that is different than the original model produced by the person ahead of them.
  - Remind the students to repeat the pattern/body percussion exactly as it was performed by the person before them. If a new rhythm is created, that only adds to the fun of the exercise.
  - Go around the entire circle, providing every student an opportunity to participate.
  - Encourage the students to keep a steady beat until everyone has a turn.
  - Challenge the students to keep going and compare the final rhythm with the original rhythm pattern.
- Once the rhythm pattern makes it around the entire circle, discuss whether or not it is identical to the original pattern.
  - If not, what changed during the trip around the circle?

Advanced Extensions

- Ideas to mix it up:
  - Add a verbal cue (such as a bell).
  - When the verbal cue sounds, the next person in the circle will immediately create a new rhythm pattern with body percussion.
- Start an additional rhythm pattern, which will sound like a canon, after the original pattern has passed through 8 students.
- Start a new pattern after only 4 students have performed the original pattern.
- Try the same process after 2 students have performed the original pattern.

Rests Rests Rests!

Teaching Ideas

- Have students chant the rhythm pattern pictured here.
- Next, guide them to step to the beat and chant the rhythm.
  - Add a 2-finger tap, while stepping and chanting.
  - Lip-sync the pattern while stepping to the beat.
- Ask a volunteer to model a physical motion that produces an audible sound.
  - Example: snap, tap, pat, clap, stomp.
- Have everyone use that motion/sound on the first and third beats – being careful to maintain silence on the rests.
  - Call on a student to find a new motion with a new sound.
- Reverse the process with silence on the beat and motion/sound on the rests.
- Invite one side of the room to produce motion/sound on the beat.
  - At the same time the other side of the room will produce motion/sound on the rests.
- Are the patterns precise or do they carry over into another part?
- Change the rhythm pattern to the one pictured below.

- Guide the students to lightly tap the new rhythm pattern with several rests.
- Divide the room into two groups.
  - Group 1 will clap the original rhythm pattern (from the beginning of this lesson) over and over.
  - Group 2 will clap the 2nd rhythm pattern.
  - Discuss the differences.
  - Have both groups clap the patterns at the same time.
  - Provide time for the groups to trade parts and clap the patterns again.

Advanced Extensions

- Ask Group 1 to move to barred instruments and play the pattern on *do* and *sol* in C Major.
    - Have Group 2 clap their rhythm pattern while Group 1 plays their pattern on the barred instruments.
    - Group 2 can add non-pitched percussion instruments to their rhythm pattern.
    - Then, allow them to trade parts and repeat the same process.
- Invite students to discuss how successful they were when playing either of the instruments.
    - Was one rhythm pattern easier to play than the other?
    - If so, why?
    - Were the rhythms clean or did some of the sounds carry over into the next beat?
    - What needs to happen for it to improve?

Partners in Common Time

Teaching Ideas

- Have everyone stand up and face a partner.
- Ask the students in each pair to decide who is Person A and who is Person B.
  - Person B will reach across and lightly tap Person A's left shoulder.
  - Person A will reach across and lightly tap Person B's left shoulder at the same time.
- Instruct the students to tap the 8th note pattern pictured above.
  - Have the students count 1 & 2 & 3 & 4 & as they tap.
  - Are they tapping together at exactly the same time?
  - Invite them to discuss how it feels if their inner pulses are not lined up perfectly together with their partner.
- Have them do the same thing again to see if they can align their tapping immediately.
- Instruct all of the students to clap and count the rhythm pattern pictured below.

- Face partners once again.
  - Person A begins by tapping and counting the 8th note subdivision.
  - Person B taps and counts the dotted quarter note/eighth note pattern.
  - Once the pairs of students appear to be settled into their rhythm patterns, instruct them to audiate and lip-sync the counting.
  - Can they stay together while they are audiating the counting?
- Go through the same process again and have the students trade parts.
  - Person B will tap the subdivision and Person A will tap the dotted quarter note/eighth note pattern.
- Have the students find a new partner as the teacher counts one free measure.
  - Start the same process over again.
  - Use an audible sound such as a bell, drum or chord played on the piano.

- When the sound occurs, the students trade parts.
- Provide several opportunities for the students to move back and forth between the two different rhythm patterns.

◆ Invite students to discuss their experiences.

- What are the differences between the two rhythm patterns?
- Which pattern serves as the subdivision?

◆ Ask the students to clap and count the rhythm pattern pictured below to review.

Advanced Extensions

◆ Isolate several measures from the students' performance literature and display them on the board.

- Instruct the students to tap and count the patterns together.
- Guide the students to locate the rhythm patterns in their performance literature.

◆ Have the teacher tap measures or phrases including the dotted quarter note/eighth note pattern.

- The students will echo the pattern by tapping.
- The students will locate the measures in the music.
- Instruct the students to sing those portions of the literature, reinforcing the dotted quarter note/eighth note pattern.

Partners in 6/8 Meter

Teaching Ideas

- Have everyone stand up and face a partner.
- Ask the students in each pair to decide who is Person A and who is Person B.
  - Person B will reach across and lightly tap Person A's left shoulder.
  - Person A will reach across and lightly tap Person B's left shoulder at the same time.
- Instruct the students to tap the 8th note pattern pictured above.
  - Have the students count 1-2-3-4-5-6 as they tap.
  - Are they tapping together at exactly the same time?
  - Invite them to discuss how it feels if one person is slower or faster than the other one.
- Have them do the same thing again to see if they can immediately tap perfectly together.
- Instruct all of the students to clap and count the rhythm pattern pictured below.

- Instruct the students to face their partners once again.
  - Person A begins by tapping and counting the 8th note subdivision.
  - Person B taps and counts the dotted quarter note pattern.
  - Once the pairs of students appear to be aligned in their rhythm patterns, instruct them to lip-sync the counting.
  - Can they stay together when they are audiating the counting?
- Go through the same process again and have the students trade parts.
  - Person B will tap the subdivision and Person A will tap the dotted quarter note pattern.

- Tell the students to find a new partner.
  - Start the same process over again.
  - Use an audible cue such as a bell, single tap of a drum or a chord played on the piano.
  - When the cue occurs, the students immediately trade parts.
  - Provide several opportunities for the students to move back and forth between the two different rhythm patterns.
- Invite students to discuss their experiences.
  - What are the differences between the two rhythm patterns?
  - Which pattern serves as the subdivision?
- Ask the students to clap and count the rhythm pattern pictured below to review.

Advanced Extensions

- Tell the students to find a new partner and decide which student is Person A and Person B.
  - Person B will tap and count the subdivision.
  - Person A will tap the other pattern.
- Have the students tap and count the two patterns in 6/8 meter.
  - When the audible cue occurs, instruct the students to change to the 4/4 rhythms from the lesson on page 10.
  - It may be necessary to review the 4/4 patterns before doing this extension.
  - Provide several opportunities for the students to tap both meters.
- Have the students trade parts.
  - Person A will tap and count the subdivision.
  - Person B will tap the other pattern.
  - Go through the same process and allow students ample opportunities to experience both meter changes.
- Invite them to do this activity without counting out loud.

Paper Plate Assessment

Teaching Ideas

- Create rhythm assessment "cards" by writing a variety of 4-beat patterns on paper plates.
- The rhythm patterns can include note and rest values that students have been working on.
- Examples are any of the measures pictured below:

- Have students review tapping and chanting each of the duration values for the notes and rests that are displayed on the paper plates.
- Guide the students to stand in a circle.
    - Pass out one paper plate to each student.
    - Tell the students to place all of the paper plates on the floor in front of them.
    - Instruct the students to silently practice the rhythm pattern in front of them.
- Ask all of the students to clap/chant their patterns at the same time.
    - Teacher will count off the preparatory measure in 4/4 meter.
    - Tell students to talk with a neighbor. They will clap their rhythm patterns for each other and check for accuracy.
    - Have the students clap their rhythm once more at the same time with the other students.
- Next, instruct the students to step to the right in front of the next paper plate in the circle.
    - Tell everyone to clap their new rhythm patterns all at the same time.
- Continue this process several times until students are comfortable with the process.
    - Have the students begin with the paper plate in front of them and continue around the entire circle without stopping until they have performed the rhythms on all of the plates in the entire circle.

- You may need to add a "free walking" measure between each plate/rhythm pattern for very young students. Example: Ta ta ta-di ta.

- As the students move around the circle, the teacher focuses on one or two paper plates with rhythm patterns that assess the success of each student as they process by.
  - Example: The teacher assesses the success of each student performing 16th notes on one paper plate strategically placed near the teacher.
  - Any note value or rest value can be the focal point, based on what the teacher wants to assess.

Advanced Extensions

- Challenge students by doing the same activity and periodically changing tempos.
- Play a recording and the students must process around the circle, while staying in tempo with the recording.
- Change the rhythm patterns on the paper plates to measures in 3/4 or 6/8 meter.
- Have students stand still.
  - Begin with one student volunteer who claps their paper plate pattern.
  - Go around the circle and have each student clap their pattern when it is their turn, in tempo, as the rhythms move around the circle.

Guessing Game

Teaching Ideas

- Have the students stand in a circle, all facing in the same direction so students are ready to march around in a circle.
  - Display a 4-beat rhythm pattern on a large card, or on the board.
  - Example: Ta ta-di ta ta-di.

  - Instruct the students to gently tap the rhythm on the shoulder of the student standing in front of them. Tap on the shoulder on the outside of the circle.
  - Go through this process several times. Use a variety of different rhythm patterns until the students are confident with the process. (Examples can be taken from the measures pictured below.)

- Have the students count off A, B, A, B, A, B, etc., around the circle.
  - Display a rhythm pattern.
  - All of the students who are "A," lightly tap the pattern on the outside shoulder of the student in front of them.
  - The person who feels the tapping will assess the "tapper's" accuracy.
  - "Thumbs up" indicates that the tapping was correct.
  - "Thumbs down" indicates that the tapping was incorrect.
- Instruct the students to turn around and face the other way, then repeat the same process with their partner.
  - All of the students who are "B," tap the pattern on a student's shoulder in front of them.
  - Their accuracy is assessed the same way, using thumbs up or thumbs down.
- Next, try this again with new partners.
  - All of the B students step just outside the circle.
  - All of the A students raise their right hand.
  - The B students step forward and pass in front of the A students raising their hands. They move to a new place in the circle, with a new partner.

Advanced Extensions

- Display the titles of 4 familiar songs. Examples: *Mary Had a Little Lamb; Twinkle, Twinkle Little Star; Row Your Boat; London Bridge.*
  - Instruct all of the A students to tap their secret rhythm on their partner's shoulder (selected from one of the songs listed above).
  - B students then guess the title of the song.
  - Change partners and have B students pat a secret rhythm on shoulders of the A students.
  - All of the A students will guess which song is the secret rhythm.
- Display a short rhythm pattern taken from one of the songs the students are working on for their performance literature.
  - Clap the rhythm pattern.
  - When the students return to their seats, challenge them to locate the song that includes the rhythm pattern.
  - Sing the phrase or section where that rhythm occurs in the song.

Pulsing Notes

(Original idea from Rodney Eichenberger and Susan Mann)

Teaching Ideas

- Have students softly chant 1-2-3-4 continuously.
- Model holding a small imaginary ball with your hands.
  - Gently "hold" the ball with the right hand on top, the left hand below it, with palms facing each other.
  - "Bounce" the imaginary ball with small pulses on each beat.
  - This represents a whole note in common time, with 4 beats.
  - After every 4 beats, reverse the placement of the hands.
  - Left hand will be on top, then after 4 beats switch to the right hand on the bottom.
  - Repeat this process for 4 measures of whole notes.
- Invite students to join as soon as they grasp the process.
- Change to half notes by chanting 1-2, 3-4 and reversing the hands on every 2 beats.
  - Repeat this process for 4 measures of half notes.
- Demonstrate quarter notes by chanting and reversing the placement of the hands on every beat.
  - Repeat this process for 4 measures of quarter notes.
- Change to eighth notes; reverse hands on every half beat.
  - Repeat this process for 4 measures of eighth notes.

- It may help younger students to tap a drum or music stand to keep a steady tempo.
  - The first time the students are introduced to this activity, it may be useful to display visual representations of the measures used for this activity.
- Call out different note values to see if the students can move immediately to the new note value.
  - Ask students to whisper the counting, then lip-sync, then audiate (think) the counting without verbalizing.

Advanced Extensions

- Invite the students to add vocalization to each note value.
  - Speak a sustained [sh] on the whole notes.
  - Speak a sustained [s] for half notes.
  - Speak [ch] on each of the quarter notes.
  - Articulate a [t] on each of the eighth notes.
- Divide the class into two groups.
  - One side of the class vocalizes and performs quarter notes.
  - At the same time, the other side of the class performs the eighth notes.
- Challenge the students in each group to listen carefully and line up their note values perfectly together so it sounds like one voice on each part.
- Next, guide the students to listen to both groups at the same time and align the quarter notes perfectly with the eighth notes, which are the smallest subdivision.
  - Trade parts and have students align the note values again.
- Continue with this process by having the students perform 2 different note values at the same time. Example: One group performs half notes and another group performs quarter notes.
- Layer on all 4 note values.
- Have students trade parts so they have an opportunity to perform all of them, always encouraging them to listen for every part.
- Perform all 4 parts as a class in the following sequence.
  - Two measures of whole notes, two measures of half notes, two measures of quarter notes and two measures of eighth notes.
  - Can they perform the sequence in a canon?
  - Try a canon 1 measure apart, then two beats apart, then 1 beat apart.

Rhythm Drills

Teaching Ideas

- Review all of the rhythm syllables used in class for note values used in common time.
  - Examples: Syllables for whole note, quarter note, eighth notes and sixteenth notes.
  - Refer to the reproducible Rhythm Elements Table on page 4.
- Divide the class into two groups and form two lines facing each other.
- The first person in both lines will compete with each other.
  - The teacher claps or taps a 4-beat rhythm in common time.
  - Example: ta ta ta-di ta.

  - The first student to write the correct stick notation on the board for the pattern wins a point for their group.
  - Continue the game so that everyone has a turn.
- After round one is completed, repeat the process.
  - Next, the teacher will clap/tap an 8-beat pattern.
  - Add dotted rhythms or syncopated rhythms.
  - Provide an opportunity for all of the students to have a turn in the game.
- The teacher can change up the game by chanting the rhythm syllables instead clapping.
  - The first student who writes the correct rhythm on the board wins the point.

Advanced Extensions

- Continue the same activity using 6/8 meter.
- Try the activity using 5/8 meter examples.
- Challenge the students by clapping alternate measures of duple meter rhythms and a triple meter rhythm.

16th Notes Deconstructed

Teaching Ideas

- Have students chant the rhythm pattern pictured above, using rhythm syllables.
  - Example: ta-ka-di-mi ta-ka-di-mi ta-ka-di-mi ta-ka-di-mi.
- Tell students to add a two-finger tap and chant the counting for the same pattern.
  - Example: 1-e-&-a 2-e-&-a 3-e-&-a 4-e-&-a.
- Instruct the students to chant the rhythm syllables or counting again.
  - For this lesson, we will focus on rhythm syllables.
  - Have them clap only when they chant the syllable "ta."
  - Continue the same process and chant the syllables and clap only on the syllable "ka."
  - Next, chant the syllables and clap only on the syllable "di."
  - Finally, chant the syllables and clap only on the syllable "mi."
  - See if the students can chant and clap the entire sequence without stopping (two measures of each syllable).
- Next, challenge the students to clap the entire sequence while audiating the rhythm syllables.
- Divide the class into two groups.
  - Group A will clap on the syllable "ta."
  - Group B will clap on the syllable "ka."
  - Try the same process with Group A clapping on the syllable "di" and Group B clapping on the syllable "mi."
- Divide the class into 4 groups, with each group clapping on a different syllable.
  - Trade parts so each group has the opportunity to perform the different syllables.
  - Invite the students to discuss why some syllables are more challenging than others.

Advanced Extensions

- Have students step on the 8th note subdivision and chant or count the rhythm syllables.
  - Begin with a slow tempo.
  - Have them clap on the syllables "ta-ka."
  - Then instruct them to clap on the syllables "ka-di."
  - Next, clap on the syllables "di-mi."
  - Finally, clap on the syllables "mi, ta."
- Invite the students to go through the entire sequence outlined here, while audiating the rhythm syllables.
  - Divide the class into two groups and have them clap different sets of syllables at the same time.
- Speed up the tempo to challenge them even more.
- Ask the students to explain how this activity coincides with dotted 16th notes they may find in their performance literature.

Which Way Are We Going?

Teaching Ideas

- Have students march to the beat and chant the rhythm syllables for the rhythm pattern pictured here.
- Next, ask them to chant the rhythm syllables and tap the rhythm pattern using two fingers in the palm of their hand.
  - Tell them to lip-sync and clap the rhythm at the same time.
- Invite the students to perform the rhythm pattern again, using a different part of their body.
- Break the class into two groups and have them clap the pattern as a canon. Each student will use their own created body percussion.
- Challenge the students to clap the pattern backwards (starting on the right and progressing to the left).
- Instruct one group to perform the rhythm from left to right, using their own body percussion.
  - At the same time, the other group will perform the pattern backwards (right to left), using their own body percussion.
  - Trade parts and have them perform the rhythm pattern again.
  - Ask the students to describe their experiences when they performed the rhythm backwards.
  - Go through the same process once again and encourage the students to create a different way to perform the rhythm pattern using the new body percussion.

Advanced Extensions

- Keep the two groups and tell them to perform the rhythm pattern again.
  - The first group performs the pattern left to right.
  - The second group performs the pattern backward, right to left.
  - The second group begins 2 measures later and performs the rhythm as a canon.

- Guide the two groups to trade parts and perform the pattern as a canon using that same process.
  - The group performing the rhythm pattern from right to left begins the canon, followed by the group performing the rhythm pattern from left to right.
  - Have the second group enter after two measures to create a canon.
- Challenge the students to perform the rhythm pattern in 3 groups.
  - The teacher designates which direction each group performs the rhythm pattern (left to right, or right to left).

Passing Rhythms Round the Circle

Teaching Ideas

- Have students form a circle.
- Next, have them clap and chant the counts for the rhythm pattern pictured here.

- Walk the students through the process of passing the rhythm around the circle.
    - Tell them to extend their right hand out to the right side and hold an imaginary tennis ball in their hand.
    - Have them use their left hand to "pick up" the imaginary tennis ball and pretend to "pass" the imaginary tennis ball from their right hand to their left hand on every eighth note.
    - Practice that motion several times while counting the rhythm pictured above.
- Next, guide the students to continue this same process, so that the imaginary tennis ball falls into their neighbor's hand on each eighth note.
    - They will pick up a new imaginary tennis ball from their neighbor on the right and continue counting and passing the ball to the left on the beat.
- Pass out tennis balls (or other small manipulatives such as bean bags, egg shakers, etc.)
    - If there are only a few manipulatives, spread them out around the circle.
    - Continue the passing game while the students count the rhythm syllables out loud.
    - Challenge them to keep a steady tempo.
    - Have the students discuss how the teamwork impacts the success of moving the manipulatives around the circle with a steady tempo.
- Play a recording of a song in 4/4 meter in a moderate tempo and have the students pass the manipulatives with the recording.
    - Instruct the students to sing one of their familiar songs while passing the items around the circle.
    - Add another layer of complexity by guiding them to change directions of the passing after every 4 measures or phrase.

Advanced Extensions

- Introduce changing meters with this activity.
- First, have the students pass items around the circle in 6/8 meter, while counting the pattern pictured below.

- Once the students have mastered that and can keep a steady tempo, have them alternate back and forth between one measure of 4/4 meter and one measure of 6/8 meter.
- Increase the complexity by introducing various other meters 2/4, 3/4, 5/8, etc.

Is It Three Or Is It Four?

Teaching Ideas

- Have the students form a circle.
- Ask them to stay in one place, step to the beat, and chant the rhythm syllables for the following measure.
  - Example: ta ta ta ta.

- Next have the students stand in place and tap their right heel to the beat.
  - Encourage them to listen carefully to "unify" their heel tapping so that is sounds like one person is tapping, rather than an entire classroom of students.
- Tell the students to turn to their right and move forward, stepping to the beat.
  - Have them chant the counting or rhythm syllables and clap on beat 1 as they move around the circle.
- Invite the students to remain in the circle and face the other direction.
- Ask them to step to the beat, in place, and chant the rhythm syllables for the following measure.
  - Example: ta ta ta.

- Guide them to snap on beat 1 as they chant the counting or rhythm syllables and move around the circle.
  - Remind the students to listen and unify their snaps to sound at exactly the same time.
  - Provide several opportunities for the students to practice counting both groups of beats.
  - Ask them to describe the difference between the two groups of beats.

- Divide the class into two circles.
    - Instruct them to audiate the counting.
    - Circle A will move and clap on beat 1 (beats grouped in 4).
    - Circle B will move and snap on beat 1 (beats grouped in 3).
    - Have both circles move at the same time.
        - If students struggle, they may need to count out loud.
        - A soft drum could also lend support.
- Change parts and go through the same process.
- Have students talk to their neighbor about this experience.
        - Was it easier to stay on track with the groups of 3 or groups of 4?

Advanced Extensions

- Continue with the two circles.
    - This time, have students clap or snap on beat 2.
    - Allow the students to experience both circles/groups of beats.
- Challenge one circle to clap or snap on beat 2 and the other circle to snap or clap on beat 3.
- Can one circle go twice as fast as the other circle?

Figure It Out!

Please refer to the Elements Table pictured on page 4.

Teaching Ideas

- Have students review all of the rhythm components pictured here.
  - Tap and chant rhythm syllables the students have previously learned.
- Divide the students into small groups of 3 or 4 students.
- Provide writing materials for each group or have them move to the board.
- Their assignment:
  - Create a 4-measure rhythm pattern in 4/4 meter.
  - Each of the individual rhythm components pictured must be used at least once. Example: quarter note, half note, sixteenth notes, etc.
  - Provide the groups sufficient time to complete their assignments.
- When the students have completed their group's rhythm pattern, go around the room and have each group perform their composition for the other members of the class.
  - Invite the students to share their observations of their peers' rhythm compositions.
- Have all of the students perform their patterns at the same time.

Advanced Extensions

- Instruct each group to trade their composition with a different group.
  - Allow a short time for silent practice.
  - Have all of the groups perform their new rhythm pattern together at the same time.
  - Continue this process until all of the groups have performed all of the rhythm compositions.
- Encourage the students to talk with the other members of their group and discuss why some rhythm compositions were more challenging than others.
- Provide one last time for the groups to perform their original compositions.
  - Challenge all of the groups to perform their original compositions. Have different groups enter after two beats, creating a canon.

CIRCLES, CIRCLES, CIRCLES

Yankee Doodle
Traditional
Yan - kee Doo - dle went to town a - rid-ing on a po - ny,
stuck a feath - er in his cap and called it Mac - a - ron - i.
Yan - kee Doo - dle, keep it up. Yan - kee Doo - dle Dan - dy,
Mind the mu - sic and the step and with the girls be han - dy!

Teaching Ideas

- Have students form two concentric circles (one circle inside the other).
- Tell students to all face to the right.
- Guide them to march forward while tapping the sternum lightly.
  - Chant, counting the beats: 1, 2, 3, 4.
- March in the other direction while chanting the text to the song.
  - Lightly tap the thighs with both hands on the beat.
- Ask the inner circle to march facing right.
  - Lightly tap the thighs with both hands on the beat.
  - Chant, counting the beats: 1, 2, 3, 4.
  - At the same time, the outer circle faces the other direction and marches while chanting the words to the song.

- Tell the students in both circles to change directions and trade parts, then repeat the same process.
- Instruct the students to talk with their neighbors and describe the differences between the two different parts.
  - One circle is keeping the beat, the other circle is chanting the text, which aligns with the rhythm.
- Assign the beat to the outer circle.
  - Have them tap the beat with two fingers and vocalize [ch] on each beat.
- Assign the rhythm to the inner circle.
  - Tell the students to lightly tap their sternum while chanting [t] on every syllable.
  - Challenge the students in both circles to march while verbalizing at the same time.

Advanced Extensions

- Ask for volunteers to name another familiar song.
  - Example: *London Bridge; Oh, Susanna*; *Twinkle, Twinkle Little Star.*
- Follow the same process with the new song.
- Have everyone begin tapping the rhythm while marching.
  - Students in each circle can either march in the same direction or opposite directions.
  - At the sound of an audible cue (drum, piano chord, whistle, etc.) have all of the students change directions at the same time and begin tapping the beat.
  - Repeat the process several times to see if the students can immediately change between beat and rhythm.

Rhythm Done Right!

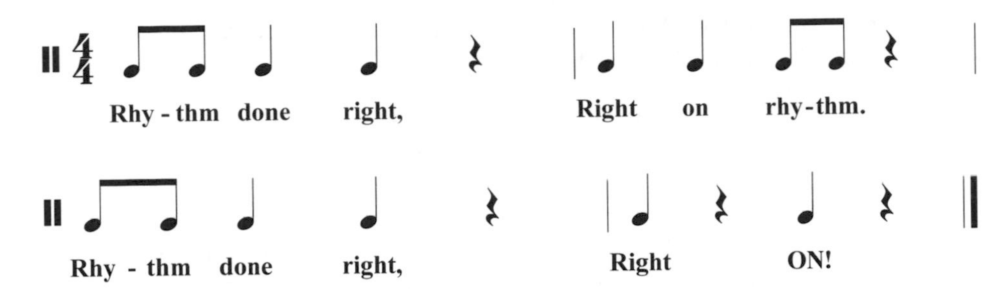

Teaching Ideas

- Tell students to chant the text and lightly tap the beat.
- Have the students chant the words while using two fingers to tap the rhythm.
- Next, have them clap the rhythm and lip-sync the words at the same time.
- Then, ask the students to lightly tap the rhythm while audiating the words.
- Change it up and ask a volunteer to create a silly voice and movement to use for the chant.
  - Have all of the students chant the text, with the new movement, using the new silly voice.
  - Lip-sync the chant using the movement only.
  - Call on several students to create various voices and movements.
  - Try imitating their movements without the voices.
- Instruct the students to speak the chant using a normal voice and clap on all of the words that begin with the letter [r].
  - Repeat the same process, only this time clap on all of the words that do *not* begin with the letter [r].
- Divide the class into two groups.
  - Have one side clap the words that begin with [r].
  - At the same time, the other side claps the words that do not begin with [r].
  - Tell them to switch parts and have them clap their assigned words once again.
  - Call on one student in each group to create body percussion to replace the clapping.
  - Invite the students to perform the two parts at the same time using the new body percussion.

Advanced Extensions

- Transfer the rhythm patterns to barred instruments.
  - Have the students perform the chant with pitched or non-pitched instrumental accompaniment.
- Break students into small groups.
  - Invite students to create their own four-line rhythm chant.
  - Have each group perform their chant for the other students in the class.
  - After each group performs the newly created chants, have the students in each group take turns teaching their chant to everyone in the class.
- Perform each of the new chants.
  - As a class, discuss which of the created chants were the easiest to perform.
  - Why were some chants more challenging than others?
  - Why were some easier to learn than others?

Circles and More

Teaching Ideas

- Have the students form a circle.
- The teacher creates a rhythm pattern using body percussion.
    - Example of rhythm: ta ta ta-di ta.

    - Body percussion is: step, step, clap-clap, step.
- One at a time, each student in the circle will echo the pattern and use the same body percussion.
    - All students will chant the rhythm syllables when they perform the rhythm pattern individually.
- Follow this same procedure.
    - The teacher will add neutral pitches or solfège syllables to the rhythm and body percussion pattern.
    - The students will echo, one at a time, around the circle.
    - Encourage the students to maintain a steady beat as the rhythm pattern progresses around the circle.
    - The teacher may want to add a drum to maintain a steady beat.
- After all of the students have had a turn, pause and take a moment to discuss how well the class kept the steady beat.
    - Did everyone echo the teacher's pattern exactly as it was demonstrated?
    - Was it easier when pitches were added or more difficult?
    - Why was it easier or more challenging?

Advanced Extensions

- Go through the same process, only assign a student to create a 4-beat rhythm pattern with body percussion.
    - Displaying a menu of predetermined rhythms may be necessary.
    - Example: only use quarter notes, quarter rests and eighth notes.
- Call on several different students to create new patterns.
    - Challenge the students to maintain the steady beat, while increasing the tempo each time a new pattern progresses around the circle.
- Divide the class into several circles and have a contest to see which circle can perform the rhythms correctly at the quickest tempo.

Duple or Triple?

Teaching Ideas

- Display flashcards or slides.
  - One card displays a 4/4, duple meter signature (pictured below).

$$\text{4/4: } ♩ \; ♩ \; ♩ \; ♩$$

  - One card displays a triple meter signature (pictured below).

$$\text{3/4: } ♩ \; ♩ \; ♩$$

- Have the students clap and chant rhythm syllables for each of the rhythm patterns pictured here.
  - Ask them to describe the differences between the two meters.
- Play short melodies on a keyboard or use recordings.
  - Play several melodies in duple meter and several melodies in triple meter.
  - Examples: *Twinkle, Twinkle Little Star*; *On Top of Old Smoky*.
- Instruct the students to tap the beat and lip-sync the counting or rhythm syllables.
  - Ask them to sit when the melody is in duple meter.
  - Have them stand when the melody is in triple meter.
  - Call on a student to create other movements to indicate the different meters.
  - Instruct the class to use the new movements to keep the beat.

Advanced Extensions

- Have the students practice "skating" around the room on paper plates.
  - Give each student two paper plates to be placed under each foot.
  - Have them practice the skating movement while counting 1, 2, 3, 4.
  - Next, ask the students to stand still on their "skates" and tap alternate legs on each beat, counting 1, 2, 3.
- Improvise a melody on a keyboard.

- Tell the students that they can only skate when they hear a duple meter.
  - When they hear the triple meter, they should alternate tapping their legs while standing still.
- Reverse the process and they can only skate when they hear a triple meter.
- Play a recording of mixed meter or improvise a melody at the piano.
  - Have the students skate the entire time, adapting their skating pattern to match the music when they hear a meter change.

Guess That Song

Teaching Ideas

- Teacher claps a rhythm of a well-known song that the students know.
    - Examples: *America; Twinkle, Twinkle Little Star* or *London Bridge.*
    - Invite the students to guess the name of the song.
    - Have all of the students clap the rhythm of the melody together.
    - If students struggle to stay together, guide them to chant the words while they clap the rhythm.
- Next ask the students to sing the song and clap the rhythm.
    - Challenge the students to hum the melody quietly and clap the rhythm.
- Finally, instruct them to lip-sync the words and tap the rhythm lightly in the palm of their hand.
    - Follow this same process for several different familiar songs.

Advanced Extension

- Write the titles of 10 familiar songs on the board.
    - Assign one student to secretly select one of the titles.
- Ask the volunteer student to vocalize/sizzle the rhythm of the secret song using an [s] or [z].
    - Call on other students to guess the name of the song.
    - Have all of the students lightly tap the beat and sizzle the rhythm of the song together.
- Repeat this process several times for different songs.

Rhythm Treasure Hunt

Teaching Ideas

- Pass out old octavos or music sheets to the students.
  - Extra octavos from reading sessions work well for this activity.
  - All of the students can have different songs, or they can all use the same song.
- Put a list of rhythm symbols on the board.
  - Example: quarter note, eighth note, quarter rest, etc.
- Instruct the students to search out those items in their music and identify the following criteria:
  - Circle all quarter notes.
  - Underline the syncopated rhythm patterns.
  - Draw a box around the whole notes.
  - Draw an "x" over every 16th note.
  - Draw a check mark above every rest.

Advanced Extensions

- This same process can be utilized to assess other music concepts such as:
  - Meter signature.
  - Key signature.
  - Ledger lines.
  - Note names.
  - Dynamic markings.

Change it Up!

Skip to My Lou

Traditional

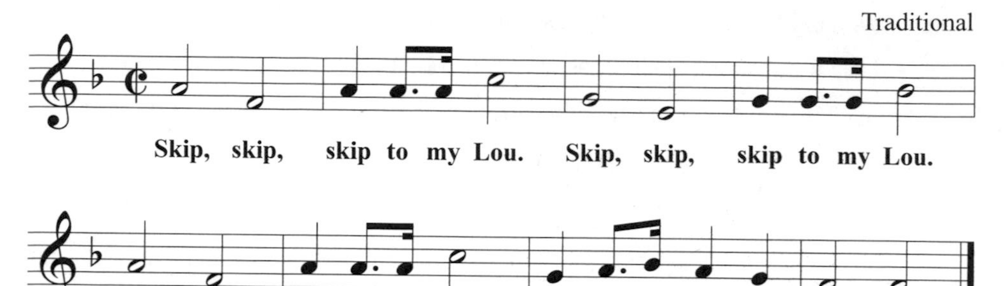
Skip, skip, skip to my Lou. Skip, skip, skip to my Lou.
Skip, skip, skip to my Lou. Skip to my Lou my dar - ling!

Teaching Ideas

- Ask students to tap the rhythm of the folk song pictured here.
  - Any familiar folk song similar to *Skip to My Lou* can work for this activity.
  - Examples: *Twinkle, Twinkle Little Star*; *London Bridge*; *Mary Had a Little Lamb*; *Yankee Doodle*; *Sweet Betsy from Pike*.
- Have them tap the rhythm again in a different order:
  - Begin with measures 7-8, then sing measures 5-6, then measures 3-4 and measures 1-2.
- Divide the class into two groups.
  - Group 1 will tap the rhythm of the song.
  - Next, Group 2 will clap the rhythm of line two, then line one.
  - Have them trade parts and perform the rhythms again.
- Instruct students to remain in the two groups.
  - Provide a few minutes for each group to create body percussion for their assigned rhythm.
  - Ask each group to perform their body percussion for the class.
  - Have both groups perform their assigned rhythm patterns together at the same time.
  - Switch parts so that Group 1 performs the rhythm from the bottom line, progressing to the top line; Group 2 performs the rhythm of the song as it is written.
  - Remind the students to use their same body percussion when they enter on the different parts.

- Allow the students an opportunity to discuss their experiences in performing the rhythm of the song in the alternate ways.
- Invite the students in both groups to create another body movement with an added verbalization, to perform the rhythm on their bodies.
  - Example: [ch], [s], [t], [boo], [k], tongue clicks, etc.
  - Have both groups perform their assigned parts at the same time.

Advanced Extensions

- Divide the students into small groups of 3 or 4 students.
- Pass out a writing utensil and 4 small cards or sticky notes to each group.
- Tell the students to select their 4 favorite measures in the song and place them one after the other. This will create a new rhythm pattern.
  - On cards or sticky notes, have one student leader in each group write out their new rhythm on the cards/sticky notes.
  - One card or sticky note contains one measure.
- Ask each group to tap and chant the rhythm syllables for the measures they selected.
- Invite the students to experiment by moving the measures around to create a new rhythm pattern.
- Have each group perform/clap their new rhythm for the class.
- Experiment by asking one group to clap their new rhythm while the other students all two-finger tap the original rhythm displayed on the board.
  - How were the two patterns similar or different?

'Tis the Rhythm to Be Simple

(sung to the tune of *Simple Gifts*)

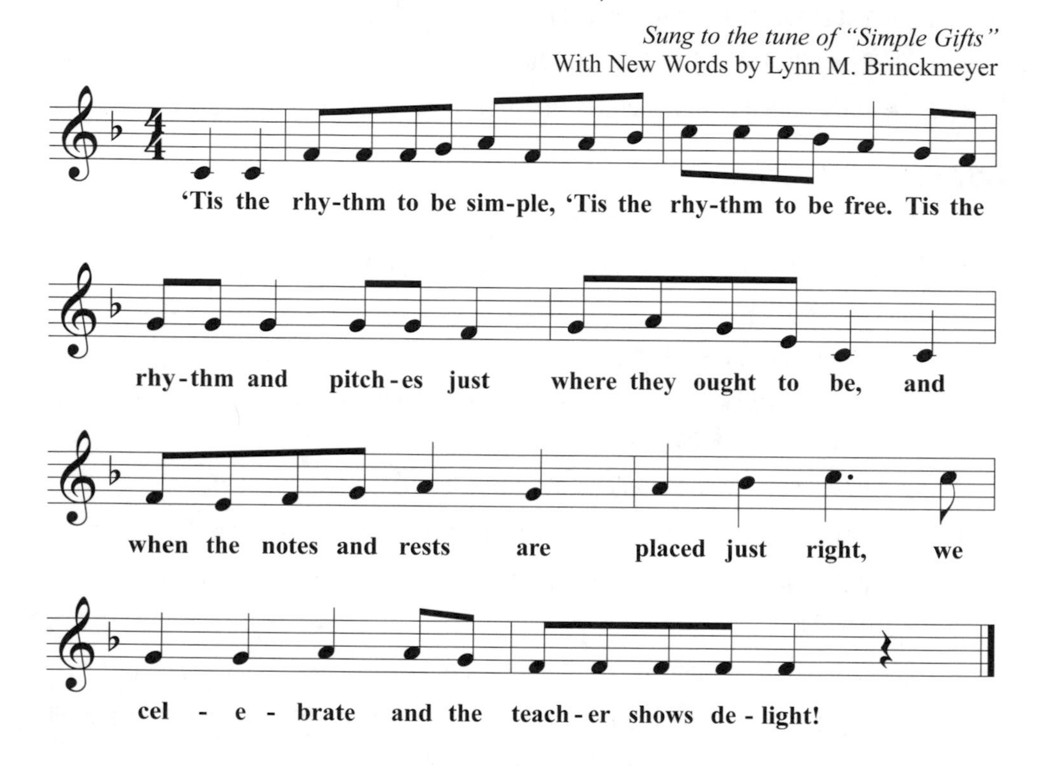
Sung to the tune of "Simple Gifts"
With New Words by Lynn M. Brinckmeyer
'Tis the rhy-thm to be sim-ple, 'Tis the rhy-thm to be free. Tis the
rhy-thm and pitch-es just where they ought to be, and
when the notes and rests are placed just right, we
cel - e - brate and the teach-er shows de - light!

Teaching Ideas

- Ask the students to chant the text while lightly tapping the beat on their thighs.
- If the melody is familiar, have the students continue tapping the beat and sing the song with the melody.
  - It may be necessary to sing the song on solfège syllables or have the teacher first model the melody for the students.
- Sing the song again and clap each time the word "rhythm" appears in the song.
- Repeat the song once more with clapping on "rhythm," and add snaps on the words "notes" and "rests."
- Challenge the students to audiate the text and perform the song using only the snaps and clapping.
  - Can they stay together?
- Have the students sing the song again.
  - Drop the clapping and snapping.

- Instead, have the students tap their foot on every word that ends in the letter [e].
- Ask for volunteers to share different ideas on how they could distinguish various words in the song.
  - Example: Tap their nose, stand up, etc.
- Incorporate the students' ideas as the class hums the song.

Advanced Extensions

- Focus on the notation of the song rather than the text.
  - Invite the students to sing the song and clap lightly on all of the 16th notes.
- Sing it again and step on all of the quarter notes.
  - Sing it through once again clapping on the 16th notes and stepping on the quarter notes.
- Instruct them to perform the song by audiating the words/melody and showing the stepping/clapping.
  - Challenge the singers to perform the song in a canon using audiation and body percussion.
  - Break into 2 groups. Have Group 2 enter after the phase "Tis the rhythm to be simple."
  - Can they perform a canon in three groups?
  - Can they perform a canon in four groups?

Playin' Rhythms in the Paw Paw Patch

Traditional Folk Song

Where, oh where is pret - ty lit - tle Mar - y?

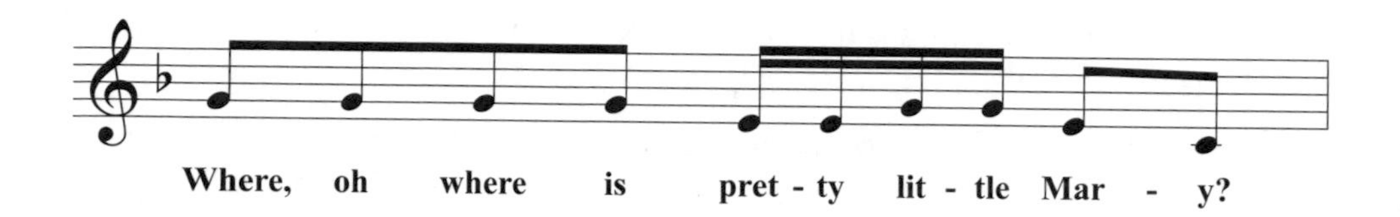
Where, oh where is pret - ty lit - tle Mar - y?

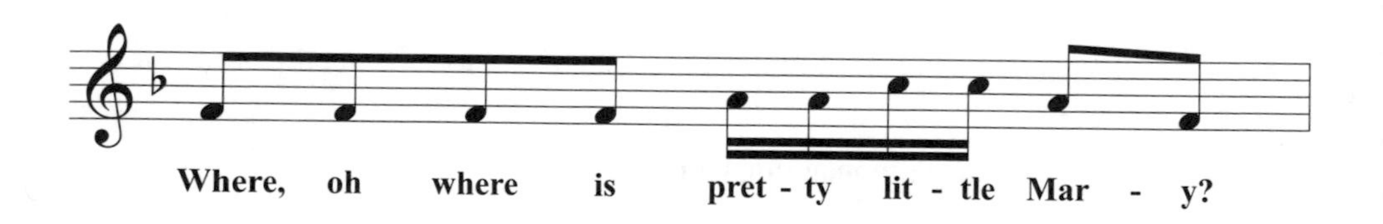
Where, oh where is pret - ty lit - tle Mar - y?

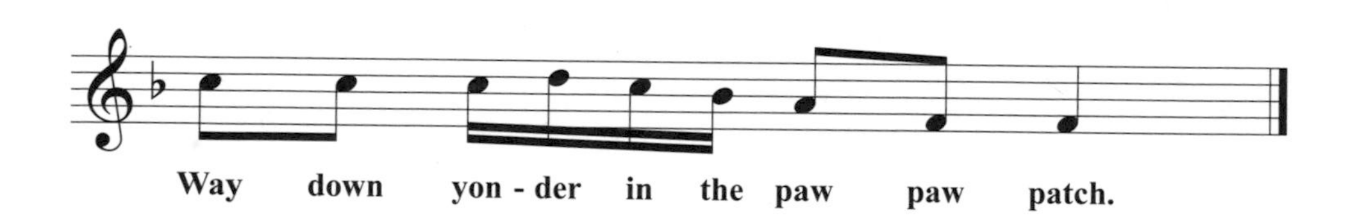
Way down yon - der in the paw paw patch.

Teaching Ideas

- Display the music.
- Have the students step to the beat and chant the words.
- Tell them to lightly tap the rhythm of the song while audiating the words.
- Guide the students to audiate the words and step on all of the 8th notes.
- Have the students do the same process again and alternately pat their legs on all of the 16th notes.
- Next tell the students to step on all of the 8th notes and pat legs on the 16th notes.
  - Add a "whoop" on the quarter notes.
- Invite the students to break into small groups and make up their own verbalizations and movements for each of the different note values.
  - Have each group perform their arrangement for the class.
  - Select one or two groups to teach their movements and vocal sounds to the other members of the class.

Advanced Extensions

- Ask a student in the class or ensemble to select one measure in the song.
  - Have them chant either rhythm syllables or counts for that measure.
  - Tell the other students that it is a race to locate that measure in song.
  - Instruct them to stand up when they locate the rhythm.
  - Continue this process with several different students counting a variety of measures.
- Pass out copies of the song *Paw Paw Patch* to every student.
- Instruct the students to write the counts under each measure.
  - Example: 1 & 2 3 4, etc.
  - The first person to finish writing the correct counts for the song is the winner.
  - This activity can be adapted to songs or sections of literature the students are learning for future performances.

Rhythms Rearranged

Scotland's Burning

Traditional

Scot-land's burn-ing. Scot-land's burn-ing. Look out! Look out!

Fire! Fire! Fire! Fire! Pour on wa - ter! Pour on wa - ter!

Teaching Ideas

- Instruct students to tap the rhythm gently on their sternum and chant the text.
- Sing the song *Scotland's Burning*.
- Direct the students to pick their favorite measure in the song.
  - Have them all clap their favorite measures at the same time.
  - Tell them to change the rhythm/note value of their favorite measure on beat 1. For example: If measure 1 is a favorite measure, change beat 1 to a quarter note.
  - Ask the class members to clap their new measures all at the same time.
  - Then, guide them to put their new rhythms somewhere on their bodies.
  - Repeat that same process for beat 2 and have them change that beat to a different note value or rest.
  - Guide them to put this new rhythm on their bodies and perform it.
- Instruct half of the class to sing the song while the other half performs their new rhythm pattern as an ostinato accompaniment.
- Reverse the process and perform the song again with the other students' improvised ostinato patterns.
- Encourage the students to pair up and compare the way they changed the rhythms in their favorite measures.

Advanced Extensions

- Challenge the students to sing the song and perform their ostinato patterns while using their improvised body percussion at the same time.
- Have the students break into groups of 3 or 4 students.
  - Guide them to experiment with the ostinato patterns they have created.
  - Have each group collaborate to create a new two-measure ostinato pattern using their ideas.
  - Let each group perform their new rhythm pattern for the class.
  - Sing the song until each group has a chance to perform their ostinato pattern for the class. Transfer the ostinato patterns to barred instruments or non-pitched percussion instruments.

Change the Beat

Sarasponda

Dutch Folk Song
Sa-ra-spon-da, Sa-ra-spon-da, Sa-ra-spon-da, Ret-set-set. Sa-ra-
spon-da, Sa - ra-spon-da, Sa - ra - spon-da, Ret-set-set. Ah -
do - ray-oh! Ah - do - ray-boom-day - oh! Ah -
do - ray-doom-day Ret - set - set. Ah-say-pa-say-oh!

Teaching Ideas

- Tell the students to put the beat in their feet and chant the text.
- Instruct them to sing the melody on a neutral syllable [lu] and gently tap the rhythm at the same time.
- Have them lightly tap the 8th note subdivision and sing the words.
- Next, tell the students to form a circle.
    - Ask them to march to the beat in a circle and sing the song again.
    - Change directions and have them march to the beat again, while singing.
    - Challenge the students to stand still and only sing the syllable on beat 1 of each measure.
        - Example: "spon"… "spon" … etc.
        - See if they can lip-sync the syllables on beat 1 of each measure, while clapping on beat 1.
        - Have them continue with the same process, only change to beat 3 of each measure.

- Challenge the students to follow the same process for beat 4 in each measure.

◆ Arrange the class into two rows facing each other (Row A and Row B).
  - Ask Row A to sing and clap the syllables on beat 1 of every measure.
  - Have Row B sing and clap the syllables on beat 3 of every measure.
  - Next have both rows perform at the same time.
  - Trade parts and perform both parts again at the same time.

◆ Encourage the students to discuss the challenges they faced during this activity.
  - Which of the beats or rhythms were easier to master?
  - Which beats or rhythms proved to be more challenging?
  - Why do you think they were more difficult?

Advanced Extensions

◆ Challenge the students to continue with a similar clapping pattern.
  - Guide them to remain standing in a circle.
  - Have the students count the beats 1, 2, 3, 4.
  - Start by having the teacher clap only on beat 1.
  - The "beats" go around the circle as the students chant the beats.
  - The next person claps only on beat 1, then the next student in the circle follows on beat 1, etc.
  - Keep the counting moving around the circle, with each student clapping on beat 1 when it is their turn.
  - Change the clapping to beat 2, moving around the circle.
  - Experiment with having the students chant/clap only on beat 3 or beat 4.
  - Challenge the students to carry on the same process, audiating the counting inside their minds rather than counting out loud.
    - It may be beneficial to lip-sync the counting. Try the same process with the words to the song.

I Have Rhythm

I have rhy - thm like Ti - to Pu-en - te!

Teaching Ideas

- Instruct the students to chant the words while stepping the beat.
- Have them chant the words over and over again.
  - Guide them to clap on the last syllable of the chant.
  - The next time through the sentence, tell them to leave off the last syllable and clap on the next to the last syllable.
  - Continue the same process until all of the syllables are taken away.
  - Example: Leave off:
    *I have rhythm like Tito Pu-en-**te!***
    *I have rhythm like Tito Pu-**en***
    *I have rhythm like Tito **Pu***
    *I have rhythm like Ti-**to***

Advanced Extensions

- Challenge the students to lip-sync the words while patting the beat lightly on the sternum.
- Invite the students to audiate the song without mouthing the words.
- Have them go through the same process outlined above and only clap on the last syllable.
  - Example: Clap on:
    *I have rhythm like Tito Pu-en-**te!***
    *I have rhythm like Tito Pu-**en***
    *I have rhythm like Tito **Pu***
    *I have rhythm like Ti-**to***
- Ask the students to share the names of their favorite popular singers, to replace the name of Tito Puente.
- Divide the class into two parts.
  - Have one group leave off the syllables starting with the end of the chant.
  - The other group will leave off the syllables starting at the beginning of the chant.
  - Try having both groups speak the chant and clap on their assigned syllables at the same.
  - Finally, ask them to do the same thing again, while audiating the words.
- This is a fun activity to use on students' birthdays.

I Like Rhythm!

My name is ________ and I like ________

She/He likes ________

Teaching Ideas

- Have the students chant the text while lightly tapping the beat on their thighs.
  - Tell them to remain silent on the rests.
  - "My name is ________________ and I like ________________."
- Guide the students to think of their favorite candy or food.
  - The teacher will demonstrate:
    - "My name is Ms. Jones and I like gumdrops."
  - The class immediately responds:
    - "She (He) likes gumdrops."
    - Younger children may need to chant the response measure twice if the students need more time to think.
  - After the group response, the next student begins immediately, sharing their name and favorite candy/food.
- Go all around the room and allow every student to have a turn.
  - The first time students participate in this activity, they may have trouble keeping the beat.
  - If a child "freezes," the class can keep tapping the beat and respond with something like the following:
    - "Her name is Rachel, her name is Rachel."
    - "His name is Tyler and he likes _______ (shrug shoulders on the rest).
- Invite the students to go around the room in the opposite direction and go through the same process.
  - Encourage them to maintain a steady pulse without slowing down or stopping.
- Display various 1-beat rhythm patterns and have the students review them by clapping and chanting the rhythm syllables.

- Example: ta; ta-di; ta-ka-di-mi; ta-di-mi; ta-ka-di.

- Use the same process as before and allow each student to speak individually.
- Instead of selecting a favorite candy/food, when it is their turn the students will clap their favorite 1-beat pattern displayed on the board.
- Example: "My name is Zack and I like ta-ka-di."
- The class immediately responds, "He likes ta-ka-di."
    - Rather than repeating the rhythm syllables out loud, the class responds by clapping the ta-ka-di pattern and audiating the syllables.

Advanced Extensions

- The teacher can switch the rhythm activity above.
    - Have each student clap their favorite rhythm pattern and the class can respond with the matching syllables.
    - Substitute other favorite items that coincide with the curriculum students are studying in other classes.
    - Examples: Countries, capital cities, animals, lakes, sports, pop stars, sports stars.
- Divide the class into two circles.
    - Move around the circle, one student at a time.
    - Instruct each student to say one word that describes this activity.
        - Examples: challenging, fun, exciting, rhythmic, fast, etc.
    - When everyone has had a turn, reverse the process and have each student describe the activity with new words.
    - Challenge the students to use no repeated words.

Make a Rhythm, Make it Now

Make a rhy-thm, make it now. Share your rhy-thm, show us how.

Teaching Ideas

- Have students tap the beat lightly on their thighs and chant the text.
- Ask the students to tell their neighbor how many beats are in each measure (4).
- Encourage them to create and clap their own 4-beat rhythm pattern.
  - Have the students clap/chant their patterns all at the same time.
- Instruct the students to chant the text.
  - Challenge them to each clap their own rhythm patterns all together immediately after the chant.
  - Move around the entire class (by rows or a circle) and allow everyone an opportunity to clap their individual pattern.
  - Example: chant, Student A claps, chant, Student B claps, etc.
- Follow the same process again.
  - Ask the students to create a different rhythm pattern.
  - Instead of clapping, they will need to create a new body percussion.
  - Encourage the students to maintain a steady tempo throughout the activity.

Advanced Extensions

- Divide the class into two groups, preferably in circles.
- Use the same process as above.
  - Begin the second circle 4 beats after the first circle.
  - Next, try having the second circle come in after 2 beats.
- Speed up the tempo to challenge students even more.
- Divide the class into 3 or 4 groups and challenge them to maintain 3 or 4 circles/parts in canon.

Secret Word - Secret Rhythm

Teaching Ideas

- Display a variety of items, or photos of items, in front of the room.
  - Example: apple, grapes, watermelon, banana, cantaloupe.
- The teacher claps the rhythm of one of the items.
  - Example: ta-ka-di-mi, or 1-e-&-a.

  - Have the students echo the clapping pattern.
  - The teacher claps the pattern once more.
  - The students clap as they chant the word.
  - Example: "wa-ter-me-lon."
- Continue this process several times.
- Invite different students to clap the secret rhythm rather than the teacher.
- To change this activity slightly, call on different students to name their favorite candy and write the names of the candies on the board (4-6 items).
  - Use the same process for clapping and identifying the different candy items selected by the students.
- Pass out writing materials to pairs, or small groups, of students.
  - Display 3 or 4 different items, photos or words.
  - Instruct the students to write the notation for the items.
  - Have the students all clap/chant the notation they wrote down to check for accuracy.

Advanced Extensions

- Use other items such as musical instruments for the activity.
  - Example: shakere, bongo, triangle, flute, clarinet, trumpet, horn, timpani.
- Substitute vocabulary words students are studying.
- Explore other areas of the curriculum the students are working on in other classes.
  - Example: names of states, countries, plants, anatomy, rivers, presidents, animals, etc.
- Invite students to use the names of their favorite pop artist or ensemble.

London Bridge Mix-Up

Traditional

Lon-don Bridge is fall-ing down, fall-ing down, fall-ing down.

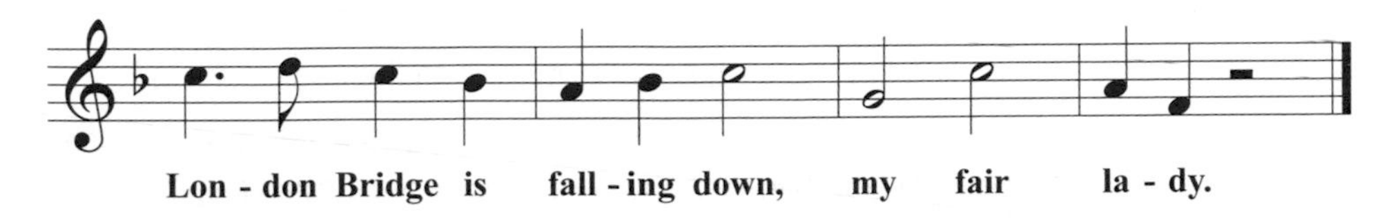
Lon - don Bridge is fall - ing down, my fair la - dy.

Teaching Ideas

- Have the students sing the song *London Bridge* and lightly tap the rhythm somewhere on their bodies.
- Ask them to sing the song again and this time, show a "thumbs up" whenever they sing a half note.
  - They should keep their thumbs down when they sing all of the other note values.
- Next, guide the students to lip-sync the words and two-finger clap only the 8th notes in their palms.
- Have them audiate the song.
  - Tell them to two-finger clap the 8th notes and show "thumbs up" on the half notes.
- Divide the class into two or three groups.
  - Challenge them to audiate with the tapping/thumbs up in a canon, entering two beats apart.
- Print the rhythm for each measure of the song on individual cards, so students can manipulate the measures.
  - Some classes may have technology that can allow students to manipulate the measures on the board.
  - Call on a student volunteer to mix up the order of the measures.
  - Have everyone clap the new rhythm pattern.
  - Do the tapping and thumbs up activity with the new rhythm.
  - Give the students several opportunities to mix up the order of the measures and tap/audiate the new rhythms.

Advanced Extensions

- Use cards with printed rhythm and pitches for each of the four measures on separate cards.
    - Sing the song on a neutral pitch [lu].
    - Call on a student to mix up the order of the cards.
- Have the students sing the new song on a neutral pitch or solfège syllables.
    - Encourage them to discuss how the song has changed.
    - Can they sing the new order of pitches and rhythms with the original words?
    - Provide several opportunities for students to mix up the order of the measures and sing their new arrangement.

About the Writer

Lynn M. Brinckmeyer

Dr. Lynn M. Brinckmeyer is Professor of Music, Associate Director for the School of Music and Director of Choral Music Education at Texas State University. During 2006-2008 she served as President for The National Association for Music Education (formerly MENC). Past offices include: President for the Northwest Division of MENC, Music Educators Journal Editorial Board, Washington Music Educators Association General Music Curriculum Chair and Conn-Selmer University Advisory Board. She also served as a Music Expert on the Disney, "Let's Play Music" Site. In addition to chairing the Eastern Washington University Music Department for six years and conducting the EWU Concert Choir, Dr. Brinckmeyer received both the PTI Excellence in Teaching Award and the CenturyTel Award for outstanding faculty. Other awards include the MENC Lowell Mason Fellow, Washington Music Educators Association Hall of Fame, the MENC Northwest Division Distinguished Service Award and Eastern New Mexico University's Outstanding Alumni Award.

Dr. Brinckmeyer recently published *Wander the World with Warm-ups!* with Hal Leonard Corporation and *Advocate for Music* with Oxford University Press. Dr. Brinckmeyer is also a contributing author for Interactive Music – Powered by Silver Burdett, The Music Director's Cookbook: Creative Recipes for a Successful Program and The Choral Director's Cookbook: Insights and Inspired Recipes for Beginners and Experts. She founded the Eastern Washington University Girls' Chorus while teaching at EWU. She also served as Artistic Director for the Idaho State Children's Chorus in Pocatello, Idaho and the South Hill Children's Chorus in Spokane, Washington. Dr. Brinckmeyer is a co-founder and Artistic Director for the Hill Country Youth Chorus in San Marcos, Texas.

Dr. Brinckmeyer's degrees include a Bachelor of Science in Education and Master of Music Education from Eastern New Mexico University, and a Ph.D. in Music Education from The University of Kansas. In New Mexico, she taught elementary music and middle school choir, then moved to higher education in the Pacific Northwest. At Texas State University Dr. Brinckmeyer teaches graduate and undergraduate courses in choral music education. She serves as Associate Director for the School of Music, Coordinator for Music Education, and directs the Texas State Women's Choir. Each summer Dr. Brinckmeyer teaches classes for Will Schmid's World Music Drumming workshops. She has conducted all state choirs and honor choirs, lectured, presented master classes and performed in forty-nine states in the United States and eighteen different countries, including China, Brazil, South Africa and Cuba.